The Tiny Book of Nature

BOOK OF KATHERINE

ISBN: 979-8-9990512-8-8

Cover photography by Pooria Shahriari and Felix Jiricka
Cover design by Book of Katherine
Back cover photo by Amith Tiwari

THE TINY BOOK SERIES
By Book of Katherine

THE TINY BOOK OF FASHION
The quick and dirty answers to fashion's
deepest questions.

THE TINY BOOK OF LOVE
Love isn't where you think you'll find it.
But it can be found.

THE TINY BOOK OF NATURE
Justice is all around us.
And court is in session.

For every action, there is an equal and opposite reaction.
Sir Isaac Newton's Third Law of Motion

CONTENTS

CHAPTER ONE
THE NATURAL LAW

No one gets away with anything. No one.

We are told, from the day we are born, that a nation's criminal justice system is the only way justice happens:

"If a bad guy is not convicted, then he got away with it."

Bullshit.

No one, but no one, gets away with murder. Or mayhem. Or greed. Or gambling.

You get the picture.

No one.

CHAPTER TWO
TRUE JUSTICE

A documentary says a woman who helped a convicted murderer escape the law for a few years is brought to a courthouse but escapes punishment.

Did anyone notice that she had cancer? Complete with a tank of oxygen and a wheelchair at court? All of her hair gone?

No. No one noticed.

Another news piece covers a pedophile who dated mothers to have access to their children, but by the time the children were ready to press charges, the statute of limitations had run out.

The journalist manages to locate the man and interview him. The interview implies the man escaped justice.

But did anyone notice that his jaw was missing? His face was mangled beyond recognition and he couldn't breathe properly.

I noticed.

A tornado strikes a small town in a very rural city. Everyone is shocked that it didn't tear up trees and farmland, but instead made a straight line across nearly 200 mobile homes. The media expresses concern and devastation.

They don't mention the child pornography ring that was being run out of that settlement.

I did.

No one gets away with anything. Ever.

It's just as dangerous as pursuing truth, because life and truth are the same.

CHAPTER THREE
CHILDREN

Everyone knows that there are laws of nature. But we don't study them all. There are far more laws in nature than we give it credit for.

When we discipline our children when they are young, we do so because we know that they will slam up against the natural law if they continue certain behaviors, and we don't want to see them suffer the consequences. We want them to be in harmony with nature, not at war with it.

For example: sharing. Sharing is part of nature. Trees cross pollinate. Bees share flowers. Creatures share dens. They have boundaries, yes, just as we all do. But when we do not teach our children to share, we are setting them up for a spanking via the natural law.

Sometimes it happens instantly. A sister,

envious of her brother's Christmas gift, steals it from him within seconds of him opening it. So he slaps it out of her arms, causing her to cry. Or a parent sees their daughter steal from their son, and puts her in time-out.

Sometimes it happens later on. A boy throws rocks at a girl during recess at school. The yard duty doesn't catch him doing it and the girl doesn't report it. But later that day, he trips and falls on the concrete, earning himself a large cut. Or perhaps, later that week, a bigger bully hears of what the boy has done and decides to throw rocks at the boy himself.

'What goes around comes around,' as they say.

There are always correlations. A cause and an effect. Start connecting the dots.

It will make you feel a lot better if you do.

CHAPTER FOUR
UNCHECKED

But what happens when a child doesn't learn to share? What happens when a parent steps in and prevents the natural law from teaching their child?

This is exactly what happens when a parent becomes upset that their child received time-out for stealing from another child and complains to the school principal. The child learns that stealing is a righteous act, and they continue to do it with greater and greater gusto.

And, since the parent steps in to circumvent the natural law, the punishments are then transferred to the parent. That's why helicopter parents are rarely happy people. They spend their lives taking on the sins of their children, which in turn teaches their children to not only continue committing heinous acts, but also teaches them to push the boundaries and commit even greater sins.

And so, the natural law slams harder and harder against the child, which forces such parents to pay greater and greater fines as they try to protect their children from nature and her lessons.

And do you know what happens in the end? In the end the parent, parents or guardian can no longer sustain the blow back. They run out of money. They run out of time. They run out of relationships. They run out of energy. They run out of health. And finally, in the end, they cannot take the blow their child has earned… and it hits the child full force.

And the poor child. They never see it coming.

They kill a friend when they crash a car while driving drunk. They end up in jail when a judge has had enough. They become homeless when their grandparents take them to court in order to kick them out. They argue with the doctor when they're told, "No. You will never play sports again."

I wonder how many parents look back when these moments arrive and wish that they had told their child why they received that time-out in the first place, all those years ago, and how to avoid receiving time out in the future.

CHAPTER FIVE
KARMA IS A BITCH

A psychologist once said that their patients often paid the price for their actions as long as two years later. They'd come to the office because their life was unraveling, but after a series of questions, the psychologist would discover that the unraveling had begun years earlier, when their patient had violated the laws of nature and thought they could get away with it.

But no. That's not the way it works.

Nature is a bitch.

If you don't listen to her first warning, her second warning or her third, fourth or fifth warnings, she'll take a bat to you. And then you look up at her and cry, "Why, mom, why!?!?"

And that's because, at the end of the day, we are all children when it comes to nature. It

is the teacher and we are the students.
If you ignore her lessons, watch out.

CHAPTER SIX
EARTHQUAKES

You might be wondering how I discovered these other laws of nature. Well, I discovered them when I began studying nature itself.

Take earthquakes. When I began studying the world's earthquakes, I noticed that certain large quakes defied the laws of nature we are taught in school. "Why," I would wonder, "is this corner of this island being hit by such large and significant earthquakes when it isn't close to volcanism or at the edge of a tectonic plate?"

And when scientific studies didn't have the answers, I looked to the area itself. I learned about the cities or the towns. I learned about the country. I learned about the culture. And then I discovered a surprising pattern: witchcraft.

On and on, these corners of the globe with

devastating earthquakes (despite local geology features that would usually indicate a stable environment) were rife with voodoo, witches, wicca and/or all other sorts of black magic.

That's when I began to watch where hurricanes, lightning and tornadoes hit.

Holy God.

There was an entire court system in the heavens that I didn't even know about. And it was pissed.

CHAPTER SEVEN
CLIMATE CHANGE…
OR APOCALYPSE?

Over the years I've found myself on both sides of the climate change debate. In the end I realized that natural disasters were indeed growing in strength and frequency, but not for the reasons climate headlines would list.

It wasn't easy. I had to read each study instead of allowing a news agency to summarize the study for me. And believe me, the studies that are so often quoted by the media regarding climate change out there — well. The studies say something else entirely.

That's been a hard lesson to learn.

But in the end, I discovered a great wealth of peer-reviewed research that painted a very clear picture of how and why our planet is going to shit. (I know. You want me to tell you all of that now. Ha! You'll just have to listen to my podcasts on the subject and dig into my research. This is not that kind of book.)

But this is what I can tell you now; it's not your buying habits that are killing the planet. It's those other habits – the one's you keep secret and hidden inside.

CHAPTER EIGHT
EXPOSED

We are taught from a young age that privacy is a concept that actually exists. In reality, privacy is simply a healthy boundary we can keep to improve various relationships between humans.

For example, a bank does not have a good relationship with its clients if it does not keep their clients' information private. The bank's entire business model fails without a privacy policy that is strictly upheld. Privacy is an essential cornerstone of the banking business.

Journaling has been proven again and again to be good for one's physical and mental health. But that research stops short when the journal isn't private. Journaling on social media – on public platforms without the boundary of privacy – can be detrimental to one's health.

But writing in a physical journal that is kept private from all others can be highly beneficial to one's health in many, many ways.

In fact, in the book *The Gulag Archipelago*, we learn how devastating it was when authorities began reading the private journals of its citizens. Sadly, today, many teachers require their students to write and turn in journal entries to be read and graded. This is an enormous violation of the natural law.

For only heaven judges a man's heart.

CHAPTER NINE
THE WATCHERS

As healthy as privacy can be, it remains a function between humans alone.

Nature? Nature sees all.

You can put a lock on your journal at night. You can use incognito mode for your searches on Google all you want. And you may fool your wife, your husband or your boss with all of your privacy screens, codes, hidden files, etc.

But when it comes to heaven, there is no such thing as privacy. Mother nature sees all. Heaven knows your heart.

You are exposed.

At all times, all of you is seen... and judged.

CHAPTER 10

GODS AND MONSTERS

"Who?" you may be asking. "Who is watching me? Who can see everything I do?"

And the simple answer is this: gods and monsters.

You see, ancient civilizations actually agree on a lot of things. For example, the story of a global flood and a man named Noah and his family who were spared can be found in 200 myths spanning nearly every continent – from east to west – from Asia to the Americas.

And, though we are told the texts contradict one another, the ancient Hebrew texts that are used in the Bible and the Torah are not so different from the paganism of Rome and Greece. Even the beloved myths of today, from Marvel Comics to J. R.R. Tolkien's Lord of the Rings – they have a lot in common too.

The only difference is the terminology.

The angels we hear about in scripture are referred to as gods in other civilizations.

And there is a hierarchy.

So, we've got the holy trinity at the top. And then we have thousands upon thousands of angels in a huge hierarchy of power. The archangels with the most power are up near the holy trinity. And the lesser angels with less power are more common and serve the angels above them, just like a company or corporation that's structured well.

A third of these angels watch us from heaven. They are the stars above. Some of them are even given rule over time, controlling the calendar year, its seasons and its months.

Another third of these angels walk the earth, gardening it – watering it – sparing us or cursing us. For their loyalty to the holy trinity, they've been given dominion over the high places – the air, the dew, the grass, the trees, the harvests and the clouds, for example.

And the final third are fallen. They have rebelled against the order of heaven. They always seek to establish a new order. And they always fail.

These dark ones rule the lower realms – the dark regions – such as underground caves, volcanoes and deep ocean ridges. They are the places we find gold, silver, plutonium, minerals, gas, oil, gemstones and more. For mankind to use any of these, they must dig down into the deep and dark realms of the fallen, and though it is not sinful to do so in and of the act itself, the temptation is always there to follow the powerful forces that rule these realms.

Think about it. When we want to get away, relax and regroup, we rarely travel to the bottom of the sea or into a dark, unlit cave. We generally refer to those places as death traps. The very thought of them can be scary. And that makes sense, knowing that fallen angels and their dark shadowy servants rule those realms.

No, when we want to experience good, we usually go to the high places, or the bright and lush places, all of which were given over to the good and faithful angels in the beginning.

Now think past vacations. Take your source of heating, for example. Have you ever noticed the difference between heat from a wood stove versus oil? One is much more healing than the other. (Hint: it's not the element ruled by the fallen.)

Ah, yes. The gods and the monsters they've created. The angels and the devils. They are here. They walk among us. They watch from above. And once we know that, the world begins to make sense again, like it did to our forefathers.

Ancient civilizations called our angels

'gods.' The two words are interchangeable in today's vernacular. But just because the words have changed doesn't mean that the gods and angels have. They exist. They always have.

And they are the true justice system on earth.

They are the Watchers.

CHAPTER 11
MERCY

There is good news. The Lord is also merciful. Nature gives us grace. We can see it all around us.

Winters may be harsh, but Spring always comes.

Tornadoes may throw hail, but rainbows follow.

Hope is in nature, just as justice is.

Right now, you might be freaking out at the thought that your private messages, your secret Only Fans account and your most shameful habits are on full display to the greatest powers in the universe.

I mean, who wants to believe that the guy struck by lightning the other day just might have been struck because of something he did!?

But that's the way it works, my friends.

That's the way it works.

But don't forget – for every 'guy struck by lightning' video out there, there are a million 'near fail' videos. When you watch a pedestrian walk right through a huge car wreck unscathed and unharmed, you are watching the angels at work.

Nothing is touched without the Lord's say so. Not even evil can touch us without the Lord's permission. That's the lesson in the Book of Job. The devil had to ask for permission every time he wanted to touch Job or his belongings.

Everything, even the devil, bends a knee in the end.

And if we do too, then sweet mercy can be ours.

CHAPTER 12

THE HEART

Until socialism, nearly every civilization on earth recognized that there are powers greater than our own. The only difference? How each culture approached that greater power.

But for the most part, blood sacrifices were offered.

Blood.

There is something about blood, isn't there?

Some say you must be redeemed by the blood of Christ in order to receive mercy from heaven. Some say you must pay religious organizations, charities and/or shrines a portion of your paycheck to gain heaven's forgiveness.

Others say you must maintain your honor.

I say you must love.

Anyone who has a relationship with love

– true love – has a relationship with heaven.
I say you must value life.
Anyone who invests in life invests in nature… and it is the living law of God.

EPILOGUE

Here is a simple, rule-of-thumb guide for behavior: Ask yourself what you want people to do for you, then grab the initiative and do it for them. Add up God's Law and the Prophets and this is what you get.

— Jesus of Nazareth

I've lived enough lifetimes to see it all. And I am so glad that, in the end, I learned about the natural law.

I was raised, like many of you, to believe that evil owns this earth and rules it. But that couldn't be further from the truth.

If it was, nothing living would be left. Earth would be scorched black, without running water, leaf or glee. The smell of sugar and cinnamon wouldn't tempt our noses nor would gifts ever be given.

Oh, evil exists, but it exists in our hearts as

well, not just the devil's. We may be made in the image of God, but my, oh my, are we evil too. We chose to be.

But we can choose differently every day.

-

When an author writes a book, it bears their signature from its beginning to its end. When a software developer writes his own program, you can see their own personal style in every line, across every section.

And creation is just like that. There is a reason a galaxy is shaped just like a hurricane, and a hurricane is shaped just like a whirlpool. There is a reason that the magnetic field of an atom, of earth, of our sun, and of our galaxy are all shaped in the same exact way: like a donut. (Technically the scientists call it a toroidal shape, but you and I know it's just a fancy way of saying 'donut,' right?)

But you get what I'm saying. Evil may be present, but it is not king. Evil may be allowed to corrupt the DNA of this planet, but it did not create the DNA itself. Just take a look at the animals! Dragonflies are ethereal and glorious. When we spot deer or horses, we stop and gaze in wonder. Clearly they weren't created by evil. But black widow spiders? Jackals? Oh, how evil corrupted DNA to make such abominations!

But evil had to merge and manipulate the

DNA that was already here to do so. And they pay the price. They paid the price in the ancient days and they pay the price today. Many types of bio-banks housing and mixing DNA across the world have faced destructive consequences in the form of floods, fires and quakes.

And there is peace in this. There is peace in knowing that justice actually happens in the world. We just aren't taught how to see it.

Since I've learned about the natural law, I have had the privilege to watch its miracles happen all around me.

Take the husband who moved in with a mistress. When he moved back home, he was offered a job interview the next day. When he blocked his mistress on Facebook and deleted all of her photos, he received a second interview from that same job.

And when he threw out all of his keepsakes from the affair, from the earring the mistress had him puncture his ear with to the matching wedding rings she bought with him to the underwear she left in his car, he was offered the job.

I've seen it work the other way too.

I watched as Mexico's cartels set fire to the innocents of Acapulco at a harrowing rate, fighting for the right to control this monster that they'd created: a trafficking port for all of North America. Oh, Acapulco. It had once been one of the most beautiful resort cities in the world.

By August of 2023, the citizens of Acapulco were caught in a war zone of terror, as every agency in Mexico's arsenal tried to lock down the bloody feud between Acapulco's many cartels. And how did the cartels react?

Blood and fire. The whole city became engulfed in smoke and innocent bystander blood as a fresh wave of violence barraged the city. Public transportation buses were toppled and torched. Well-known business owners were slaughtered. Young girls were found dead on the side of the highway.

So a Category-5 Hurricane erased Acapulco from the map that October. It gave no warning. It developed in secret. It broke all records. And it hit in the middle of the night – midnight, to be exact.

You won't find footage of Hurricane Otis. It was gone by dawn.

All you'll find are the shells of what were once beach-front apartments. Every window is gone. Every apartment is empty. There is no furniture. There are no appliances. And the streets are just as empty.

Weather analysts were shocked to see a hurricane along the Pacific coast. But they were even more shocked to see it develop from a Category-1 hurricane into a Category-5 hurricane in just 12 hours... leaving the residents of Acapulco completely unaware of it until it was too late.

It struck in the dead of night.

The Book of Enoch says that storms like these are angels themselves. I believe it. That storm had one hell of an intelligence. It was out for blood and justice.

And it got it.

I myself am a miracle. The doctors told my husband and I to prepare for the worst. Most never expected me to walk again. My symptoms were too severe. My paralysis was too far and wide. And my muscles were too weak to recover.

And yet here I am. I just attended an off-Broadway play. Oh, yes. I needed to sit in the handicap section. Oh, yes. I was the only one with a walker. But I sat amongst the living and the healthy for once.

And my doctors are in awe.

Did this miracle come easily? No. It's been a very painful journey back from the edge of death. But! There is a great deal of evidence to suggest that my choices while deathly-ill played a role in my recovery.

The greater the pain, the harder I chased truth. The more my limbs became unresponsive and unfeeling, the more avenues I found to continue learning, seeking and writing. And when I couldn't find anyone like myself online, I did what I would want someone else to do for me: I tried to be a light to those trapped in the dark, in whatever way

I could.

This week my physical therapist taught me how to walk heel-toe again. She is a mean, mean woman. It has been painful AF. But I'm doing it. I'm walking taller and without a walker as a result – on my way to full-functionality – I hope.

(She is not *really* mean. She is the absolute best. I was very, very blessed to have her, you know.)

In the past, I would say that my journey could not be explained. Evil would want me trapped in bed, eventually dead. But evil doesn't rule this world. That's why we pray, "Your will be done, on earth as it is in heaven."

Invite heaven into your world, and see what comes… come what may.

ACKNOWLEDGEMENTS

In a word, what I'm saying is, 'Grow up.' You're kingdom subjects. Now live like it. Live your God-created identity. Live generously and graciously toward others, the way God lives toward you.

-Jesus of Nazareth

I spent far too much of my life living out my other identity, the one they molded me into. In the depths of my illness, I decided to seek out who *they* were.

'They' want us to do this.

'They' want us to do that.

'They' make the laws, not us.

They, they, they, they…

Who the hell are we referring to when we say *they*!?

It took years of hunting down primary sources, and then following them up the chain of command. And in the end I discovered that *they* are the fallen angels and their human followers (whom I now call death eaters, honestly, with so many carrying a very real snake tattoo on their inner arms and all).

They are found in every culture and work in tandem far more than anyone realizes.

But here's what else I learned; they are the minority.

Only one third of the angels fell. The other two thirds are faithful to the natural law.

And this discovery really changed my life.

So this book is dedicated to these angels who have stayed true – who still love and live the natural law. They have helped me discover my God-created identity while helping me kill off the false one I'd been given. And becoming the one I was created to be has unlocked a deep joy within me that I will never be able to fully describe – but my God, is it blazing with glory and wonderful light!

And this is because of you, the two-thirds who fight evil and the ones who live in harmony with you – I give you my thanks.

When I have asked in silence, too broken to speak, you have answered. When I have cried in the dark, overwhelmed and afraid, you have soothed. And when I have despaired in the cold, wondering if I was forsaken, you have surprised me with miracles of delight that I have never, ever earned or deserved.

Oh, my dearest angels above, beyond and beside – I would not be alive without you.

And oh! My dearest and most beloved family. You who read my words in the middle of the night, who shared my thoughts at dawn's first light, who translated faithfully for so many of us across the globe, who protected me and my name, even to this day – to these friends of mine who held my hand as I walked through the valley of death – no matter where you were in the world – without you I never would've discovered these realms.

Without your patience, without your peace, without your trust and your curiosity, would I have ever discovered the angels that surrounded me? No. You are my first family.

When I asked you to send love, you did and I was lifted up. When a procedure did not go well, you sent prayers and I was healed. You have been my reason for fighting past the pain… and you have been the wind in my sails as I have sought truth in every corner of the world.

I have always said that we make the best team. I do research for you and you send love to me. And together we are the world's greatest secret, I think.

These three books, *The Tiny Book of Fashion*, *The Tiny Book of Love* and *The Tiny Book of Nature,* would not exist without you. It has been an honor and a pleasure to finally meet you.

For our work together has broken expectations. I am able to venture out into the world once more. And you are there. I love talking with you.

It is a pleasure I wasn't sure I'd ever taste. And it is everything.

And to my Lord, Savior and Healer, I will always bend a knee to you for all of eternity. My song is dedicated to you.

Book of Katherine
August 17, 2025
9:12 p.m.

www.ingramcontent.com/pod-product-compliance
Lightning Source LLC
Chambersburg PA
CBHW021120020426
42331CB00004B/558